TIME AND MATERIALS

TIME AND
MATERIALS

POEMS

1997–2005

ROBERT HASS

An Imprint of HarperCollins Publishers

ACKNOWLEDGMENTS

Some of these poems appeared in *American Poetry Review, Colorado Quarterly, Environmen-tal Action Committee of West Marin Newsletter, Los Angeles Times Book Review, New American Writing, Pequod, Two Lines,* and *Volt.* Thanks to the editors. "State of the Planet" was commis-sioned by the Lamont-Doherty Earth Observatory at Columbia University and first appeared, in somewhat different form, in "Science," a section of the *New York Times.* "A Swarm of Dawns, A Flock of Restless Noons," "Futures in Lilacs," "Etymology," "The World as Will and Representation," "Breach and Orison," and "Art and Life" first appeared in *Photographers, Writers, and the American Scene: Visions of Passage,* ed. James L. Enyeart, Areana Editions, 2002. "Time and Materials" first appeared in *Richter 868: Eight Abstract Pictures,* ed. David Breskin, San Francisco Museum of Modern Art, 2002. "Horace: Three Imitations" began as translations for *The Odes of Horace,* ed. J. D. McClatchy, Farrar Straus, 2001. "Then Time," "The Problem of Describing Color," and "The Problem of Describing Trees" first appeared in the *The New Yorker.* I need to thank the Lannan Foundation and the Whiting Foundation for the gift of time in which some of this work was done.

HarperCollins books may be purchased for educational, business, or sales promo-tional use. For information please write: Special Markets Department, HarperCollins Publishers, 10 East 53rd Street, New York, NY 10022.

A hardcover edition of this book was published in 2007 by Ecco, an imprint of HarperCollins Publishers.

FIRST PAPERBACK EDITION

Designed by Gretchen Achilles

The Library of Congress has catalogued the hardcover edition as follows:

Hass, Robert.
Time and materials: poems, 1997–2005/Robert Hass. — 1st ed.
p. cm.
ISBN 978-0-06-134960-7
I. Title.
PS3558.A725T56 2007
811'.54–dc22   2007030294

ISBN 978-0-06-135028-3 (pbk.)

10   11   12   ID/RRD   10   9   8   7   6   5   4   3   2

CONTENTS

TIME AND MATERIALS

IOWA, JANUARY

In the long winter nights, a farmer's dreams are narrow.
Over and over, he enters the furrow.

AFTER TRAKL

October night, the sun going down,
Evening with its brown and blue
(Music from another room),
Evening with its blue and brown.
October night, the sun going down.

ENVY OF OTHER PEOPLE'S POEMS

In one version of the legend the sirens couldn't sing.
It was only a sailor's story that they could.
So Odysseus, lashed to the mast, was harrowed
By a music that he didn't hear—plungings of sea,
Wind-sheer, the off-shore hunger of the birds—
And the mute women gathering kelp for garden mulch,
Seeing him strain against the cordage, seeing
The awful longing in his eyes, are changed forever
On their rocky waste of island by their imagination
Of his imagination of the song they didn't sing.

A SUPPLE WREATH OF MYRTLE

Poor Nietzsche in Turin, eating sausage his mother
Mails to him from Basel. A rented room,
A small square window framing August clouds
Above the mountain. Brooding on the form
Of things: the dangling spur
Of an Alpine columbine, winter-tortured trunks
Of cedar in the summer sun, the warp in the aspen's trunk
Where it torqued up through the snowpack.

"Everywhere the wasteland grows; woe
To him whose wasteland is within."

Dying of syphilis. Trimming a luxuriant mustache.
In love with the opera of Bizet.

"Tender little Buddha," she said
Of my least Buddha-like member.
She was probably quoting Allen Ginsberg,
Who was probably paraphrasing Walt Whitman.
After the Civil War, after the death of Lincoln,
That was a good time to own railroad stocks,
But Whitman was in the Library of Congress,
Researching alternative Americas,
Reading up on the curiosities of Hindoo philosophy,
Studying the etchings of stone carvings
Of strange couplings in a book.

She was taking off a blouse,
Almost transparent, the color of a silky tangerine.
From Capitol Hill Walt Whitman must have been able to see
Willows gathering the river haze
In the cooling and still-humid twilight.
He was in love with a trolley conductor
In the summer of—what was it?—1867? 1868?

THREE DAWN SONGS IN SUMMER

1.

The first long shadows in the fields
Are like mortal difficulty.
The first birdsong is not like that at all.

2.

The light in summer is very young and wholly unsupervised.
No one has made it sit down to breakfast.
It's the first one up, the first one out.

3.

Because he has opened his eyes, he must be light
And she, sleeping beside him, must be the visible,
One ringlet of hair curled about her ear.
Into which he whispers, "Wake up!"
"Wake up!" he whispers.

THE DISTRIBUTION OF HAPPINESS

Bedcovers thrown back,
Tangled sheets,
Lustrous in moonlight.

Image of delight,
Or longing,
Or torment,

Depending on who's
Doing the imagining.

(I know: you are the one
Pierced through, I'm the one
Bent low beside you, trying
To peer into your eyes.)

ETYMOLOGY

Her body by the fire
Mimicked the light-conferring midnights
Of philosophy.
Suppose they are dead now.
Isn't "dead now" an odd expression?
The sound of the owls outside
And the wind soughing in the trees
Catches in their ears, is sent out
In scouting parties of sensation down their spines.
If you say it became language or it was nothing,
Who touched whom?
In what hurtle of starlight?
Poor language, poor theory
Of language. The shards of skull
In the Egyptian museum looked like maps of the wind-eroded
Canyon labyrinths from which,
Standing on the verge
In the yellow of a dwindling fall, you hear
Echo and re-echo the cries of terns
Fishing the worked silver of a rapids.
And what to say of her wetness? The Anglo-Saxons
Had a name for it. They called it *silm*.
They were navigators. It was also
Their word for the look of moonlight on the sea.

THE PROBLEM OF
DESCRIBING COLOR

If I said—remembering in summer,
The cardinal's sudden smudge of red
In the bare gray winter woods—

If I said, red ribbon on the cocked straw hat
Of the girl with pooched-out lips
Dangling a wiry lapdog
In the painting by Renoir—

If I said fire, if I said blood welling from a cut—

Or flecks of poppy in the tar-grass scented summer air
On a wind-struck hillside outside Fano—

If I said, her one red earring tugging at her silky lobe,

If she tells fortunes with a deck of fallen leaves
Until it comes out right—

Rouged nipple, mouth—

(How could you not love a woman
Who cheats at the Tarot?)

Red, I said. Sudden, red.

THE PROBLEM OF DESCRIBING TREES

The aspen glitters in the wind
And that delights us.

The leaf flutters, turning,
Because that motion in the heat of August
Protects its cells from drying out. Likewise the leaf
Of the cottonwood.

The gene pool threw up a wobbly stem
And the tree danced. No.
The tree capitalized.
No. There are limits to saying,
In language, what the tree did.

It is good sometimes for poetry to disenchant us.

Dance with me, dancer. Oh, I will.

Mountains, sky,
The aspen doing something in the wind.

WINGED AND ACID DARK

A sentence with "dappled shadow" in it.
Something not sayable
spurting from the morning silence,
secret as a thrush.

The other man, the officer, who brought onions
and wine and sacks of flour,
the major with the swollen knee,
wanted intelligent conversation afterward.
Having no choice, she provided that, too.

Potsdamerplatz, May 1945.

When the first one was through he pried her mouth open.
Bashō told Rensetsu to avoid sensational materials.
If the horror of the world were the truth of the world,
he said, there would be no one to say it
and no one to say it to.
I think he recommended describing the slightly frenzied
swarming of insects near a waterfall.

Pried her mouth open and spit in it.
We pass these things on,
probably, because we are what we can imagine.

Something not sayable in the morning silence.
The mind hungering after likenesses. "Tender sky," etc.,
curves the swallows trace in air.

A SWARM OF DAWNS,
A FLOCK OF RESTLESS NOONS

There's a lot to be written in the Book of Errors.
The elderly redactor is blind, for all practical purposes,

He has no imagination, and field mice have gnawed away
His source text for their nesting. I loved you first, I think,

When you stood in the kitchen sunlight and the lazy motes
Of summer dust while I sliced a nectarine for Moroccan salad

And the seven league boots of your private grief. Maybe
The syntax is a little haywire there. Left to itself,

Wire must act like Paul Klee with a pencil. *Hay*
Is the Old English word for *strike*. You strike down

Grass, I guess, when it is moan. Mown. The field mice
Devastated the monastery garden. Maybe because it was summer

And the dusks were full of marsh hawks and the nights were soft
With owls, they couldn't leave the herbs alone: gnawing the roots

Of rosemary, nibbling at sage and oregano and lemon thyme.
It's too bad *eglantine* isn't an herb, because it's a word

I'd like to use here. Her coloring was a hybrid
Of rubbed amber and the little flare of dawn rose in the kernel

Of an almond. It's a wonder to me that I have fingertips.
The knife was very sharp. The scented rose-orange moons,

Quarter moons, of fruit fell to the cutting board
So neatly it was as if two people lived in separate cities

And walked to their respective bakeries in the rain. Her bakery
Smelled better than his. The sour cloud of yeast from sourdough

Hung in the air like the odor of creation. They both bought
Sliced loaves, they both walked home, they both tripped

In the entry to their separate kitchens, and the spilled slices
Made the exact same pattern on the floor. The nectarines

Smelled like the Book of Luck. There was a little fog
Off the bay at sundown in which the waning moon swam laps.

The Miwoks called it Moon of the Only Credit Card.
I would have given my fingertips to touch your cheekbone,

And I did. That night the old monk knocked off early. He was making it
All up anyway, and he'd had a bit of raisin wine at vespers.

BREACH AND ORISON

I. TERROR OF BEGINNINGS

What are the habits of paradise?
It likes the light. It likes a few pines
on a mass of eroded rock in summer.

You can't tell up there if rock and air
are the beginning or the end.

What would you do if you were me? she said.

If I were you-you, or if I were you-me?

If you were me-me.

If I were you-you, he said, I'd do exactly
what you're doing.

—All it is is sunlight on granite.
Pines casting shadows in the early sun.

Wind in the pines like the faint rocking
of a crucifix dangling
from a rearview mirror at a stopsign.

2. THE PALMER METHOD

The answer was
the sound of water, *what*

what, what, the sprinkler
said, the question

of resilvering the mirror
or smashing it

once and for all the
tea in China-

town getting out of this film
noir intact or—damaged

as may be—with tact
was not self-evident

(they fired the rewrite man).
Winters are always touch

and go, it rained,
it hovered on the cusp

between a *drizzle*
and a *shower,* it was

a reverie and inconsolable.
There but for the grace

of several centuries
of ruthless exploitation,

we said, hearing
rumors, or maybe whimpers

from the cattle car—
the answer was within

a radius of several
floor plans for the house

desire was always building
and destroying, the

produce man misted
plums and apple-pears

the color of halogen
streetlamps in a puddle.

They trod as carefully
as haste permitted,

she wept beside him
in the night.

Maybe if I made the bed,
it would help. Would the modest diligence
seem radiant, provoke a radiance?
(Outside aspens glittering in the wind.)

If I saw the sleek stroke of moving darkness
was a hawk, high up, nesting
in the mountain's face, and if,
for once, I didn't want to be the hawk,
would that help? Token of earnest,
spent coin of summer, would the wind
court me then, and would that be of assistance?

The woman who carries the bowl
bows low in your presence, bows to the ground.
It doesn't matter what she's really thinking.
Compassion is formal. Suffering is the grass.
She is not first thought, not the urgency.

The man made of fire drinks. The man
made of cedar drinks.

Two kinds of birds are feasting in the cottonwoods.
She sprinkles millet for the ones that feast on grief.
She strews tears for the thirsty ones
desire draws south when the leaves begin to turn.

THE WORLD AS WILL AND REPRESENTATION

When I was a child my father every morning—
Some mornings, for a time, when I was ten or so,
My father gave my mother a drug called antabuse.
It makes you sick if you drink alcohol.
They were little yellow pills. He ground them
In a glass, dissolved them in water, handed her
The glass and watched her closely while she drank.
It was the late nineteen-forties, a time,
A social world, in which the men got up
And went to work, leaving the women with the children.
His wink at me was a nineteen-forties wink.
He watched her closely so she couldn't "pull
A fast one" or "put anything over" on a pair
As shrewd as the two of us. I hear those phrases
In old movies and my mind begins to drift.
The reason he ground the medications fine
Was that the pills could be hidden under the tongue
And spit out later. The reason that this ritual
Occurred so early in the morning—I was told,
And knew it to be true—was that she could,
If she wanted, induce herself to vomit,
So she had to be watched until her system had
Absorbed the drug. Hard to render, in these lines,
The rhythm of the act. He ground two of them
To powder in a glass, filled it with water,
Handed it to her, and watched her drink.
In my memory, he's wearing a suit, gray,
Herringbone, a white shirt she had ironed.
Some mornings, as in the comics we read
When Dagwood went off early to placate
Mr. Dithers, leaving Blondie with crusts
Of toast and yellow rivulets of egg yolk
To be cleared before she went shopping—

On what the comic called a shopping spree—
With Trixie, the next-door neighbor, my father
Would catch an early bus and leave the task
Of vigilance to me. "Keep an eye on Mama, pardner."
You know the passage in the *Aeneid*? The man
Who leaves the burning city with his father
On his shoulders, holding his young son's hand,
Means to do well among the flaming arras
And the falling columns while the blind prophet,
Arms upraised, howls from the inner chamber,
"Great Troy is fallen. Great Troy is no more."
Slumped in a bathrobe, penitent and biddable,
My mother at the kitchen table gagged and drank,
Drank and gagged. We get our first moral idea
About the world—about justice and power,
Gender and the order of things—from somewhere.

My friend's older sister's third husband's daughter—
That's about as long as a line of verse should get—
Karmic debris? A field anthropologist's kinship map?
Just sailed by me on the Berkeley street. A student
Of complex mathematical systems, a pretty girl,
Ash-blond hair. I could have changed her diapers.
And that small frown might be her parents' lives.
Desire that hollows us out and hollows us out,
That kills us and kills us and raises us up and
Raises us up. Always laughable from the outside:
The English wit who complained of sex that the posture
Was ridiculous had not been struck down by the god
Or goddess to whose marble threshing floor offerings
Of grapes or olive boughs and flowers or branches
Laden with new fruit or bundles of heavy-headed wheat
Were brought as to any other mystery or power.
My friend sat on the back steps on a summer night
Sick with her dilemma, smoking long cigarettes
While bats veered in the dark and the scraping sound
Of a neighbor cleaning a grill with a wire brush
Ratcheted steadily across the backyard fence.
"He's the nicest man I could imagine," she had said,
"And I feel like I'm dying." Probably in her middle thirties
Then. Flea markets on Saturday mornings, family dinners
On Sunday, a family large enough so that there was always
A birthday, a maiden aunt from the old neighborhood
In San Francisco, or a brother-in-law, or some solemn child
Studying a new toy in silence on the couch.
Had not lived where, tearing, or like burnished leaves
In a vortex of wind, the part of you that might observe
The comedy of gasps and moans gives way, does not
Demur. Though she did laugh at herself. An erotic
Attachment one whole winter to the mouth

Of a particular television actor—she'd turn the TV on—
Watch him for a minute with a kind of sick yearning—
Shake her head—turn the TV off—go back to the translation
Of Van Gogh's letters which was her project that year—
Or do some ironing—that always seemed to calm her—
The sweet iron smell of steam and linen. "Honest to God,"
She'd say, an expression the elderly aunts might have used,
"For Pete's sake," she'd say, "get yourself together."
Hollow flute, or bell not struck, sending out a shimmering
Not-sound, in waves and waves, to the place where the stunned dead
In the not-beginning are gathered to the arms of the living
In the not-noon: the living who grieve, who rage against
And grieve the always solicited, always unattended dead
In the tiered plazas or lush meadows of their gathered
Absence. A man wants a woman that way. A person a person.
Down on all fours, ravenous and humbled. And later—
"Lovers, you remember the shoeshine boys in Quito
In the city market? Missing teeth, unlaced tennis shoes.
They approach you smiling. Their hands are scrofulous,
They have no rules, and they'll steal anything and so
Would you if you were they." The old capital has always
Just been sacked, the temple hangings burned, and peasants
In the ruins are roasting the royal swans in a small fire
Coaxed from the sticks of the tax assessor's Empire chair
Up against a broken wall. Lent: the saints' bodies
Dressed in purple sacks to be taken off at Easter.
For Magdalen, of course, the resurrection didn't mean
She'd got him back. It meant she'd lost him in another way.
It was the voice she loved, the body, not the god
Who, she had been told, ascended to his heaven,
There to disperse tenderness and pity on the earth.

FOR CZESŁAW MIŁOSZ IN KRAKÓW

The fog has hovered off the coast for weeks
And given us a march of brilliant days
You wouldn't recognize—who have grumbled
So eloquently about gray days on Grizzly Peak—
Unless they put you in mind of puppet pageants
Your poems remember from Lithuanian market towns
Just after the First World War. Here's more theater:
A mule-tail doe gave birth to a pair of fawns
A couple of weeks ago just outside your study
In the bed of oxalis by the redwood trees.
Having dropped by that evening, I saw,
Though at first I couldn't tell what I was seeing,
A fawn, wet and shivering, curled almost
In a ball under the thicket of hazel and toyon.
I've read somewhere that does hide the young
As best they can and then go off to browse
And recruit themselves. They can't graze the juices
In the leaves if they stay to protect the newborns.
It's the glitch in engineering through which chance
And terror enter on the world. I looked closer
At the fawn. It was utterly still and trembling,
Eyes closed, possibly asleep. I leaned to smell it:
There was hardly a scent. She had licked all traces
Of the rank birth-smell away. Do you remember
This fragment from Anacreon?—the context,
Of course, was probably erotic: " . . . her gently,
Like an unweaned fawn left alone in a forest
By its antlered mother, frail, trembling with fright."
It's a verse—you will like this detail—found
In the papyrus that wrapped a female mummy
A museum in Cairo was examining in 1956.
I remember the time that a woman in Portland
Asked if you were a reader of Flannery O'Connor.

You winced regretfully, shook your head,
And said, "You know, I don't agree with the novel."
I think you haven't agreed, in this same sense,
With life, never accepted the cruelty in the frame
Of things, brooded on your century, and God the Monster,
And the smell of summer grasses in the world
That can hardly be named or remembered
Past the moment of our wading through them,
And the world's poor salvation in the word. Well,
Dear friend, you resisted. You were not mute.
Mark tells me he has seen the fawns grazing
With their mother in the dusk. Gorging on your roses—
So it seems they made it through the night
And neither dog nor car has got to them just yet.

TIME AND MATERIALS

Gerhard Richter: Abstrakt Bilden

1.

To make layers,
As if they were a steadiness of days:

It snowed; I did errands at a desk;
A white flurry out the window thickening; my tongue
Tasted of the glue on envelopes.

On this day sunlight on red brick, bare trees,
Nothing stirring in the icy air.

On this day a blur of color moving at the gym
Where the heat from bodies
Meets the watery, cold surface of the glass.

Made love, made curry, talked on the phone
To friends, the one whose brother died
Was crying and thinking alternately,
Like someone falling down and getting up
And running and falling and getting up.

2.

The object of this poem is not to annihila

To not annih

The object of this poem is to report a theft,
    In progress, of everything

That is not these words
  And their disposition on the page.

The object o   f this poem is to report a theft,
  In progre   ss of everything that exists
That is not th   ese words
  And their d   isposition on the page.

The object of his poe is t   epor   a theft
  In   rogres f ever   hing   at   xists
Th   is no   ese   w rds
  And their disp sit on o   the pag

3.

To score, to scar, to smear, to streak,
To smudge, to blur, to gouge, to scrape.

"Action painting," i.e.,
The painter gets to behave like time.

4.

The typo would be "paining."

(To abrade.)

5.

Or to render time and stand outside
The horizontal rush of it, for a moment
To have the sensation of standing outside
The greenish rush of it.

6.

Some vertical gesture then, the way that anger
Or desire can rip a life apart,

Some wound of color.

ART AND LIFE

You know that milkmaid in Vermeer? Entirely absorbed
In the act of pouring a small stream of milk—
Shocking in the Mauritshuis Museum in The Hague
To have seen how white it is, and alive, as seeing people
Reading their poetry or singing in a chorus, you think
You see the soul is an animal going about its business,
A squirrel, its coat sheening toward fall, stretching
Its body down a slim branch to gather one ripe haw
From a hawthorne, testing the branch with its weight,
Stilling as it sinks, then gingerly reaching out a paw.
There is nothing less ambivalent than animal attention
And so you honor it, admire it even, that her attention,
Turned away from you, is so alive, and you are melancholy
Nevertheless. It is best, of course, to be the one engaged
And being thought of, to be the pouring of the milk.
In The Hague, in the employee's cafeteria, I wondered
Who the restorer was. The blondish young woman
In the boxy, expensive Japanese coat picking at a dish
Of cottage cheese—cottage cheese and a pastry? The sugar
On the bun, long before she woke up, had suffered
Its transformation in the oven. She seems to be a person
Who has counted up the cost and decided what to settle for.
It's in the way her soft, abstracted mouth
Receives the bits of bread and the placid sugars.
Or the older man, thinning brown hair, brown tweed coat,
Brown buckskin shoes like the place where dust and sunset
Meet and disappear. A mouth formed by private ironies,
As if he'd sat silent in too many meetings with people
He thought more powerful and less intelligent than he.
Or the whip-thin guy with black, slicked-back hair
And a scarified zigzag flash of lightning at the temple?
I didn't know if there was a type. I wanted
To interview her, or him. What do you do with your life?

I am an acolyte. I peel time, with absolute care,
From thin strips of paint on three hundred year old canvas.
I make the milk milk that flows from the gray-brown paint
Of a pitcher held by a represented woman, young, rose
And tender yellow for the cheek the light is lucky enough
To seem to touch, by a certain window that refracts it.
I am the servant of a gesture so complete, a body
So at peace, it has become a thought, entirely its own,
And, though it stills desire, infinitely to be desired,
Though neither known nor possessed by you
Or anyone else. The man in black must be an assistant curator.
He looks like he thinks he is a work of art. Everywhere
In The Hague the low-lying smell of sea salt.
We don't know a thing about the mother of Vermeer.
Obviously he displaced her nipple there, took
The whole Madonna tradition and turned it into light and milk
By some meticulous habit of mind the geometries
Of composition worked in him. And her: strong Dutch body,
Almost tender light, the plainness of the room,
The rich red rug her skin, reddened a little
From the roughness of a towel perhaps, picks up.
And the upward thrust of what longing stirs in you
Toward what dark and what dazed, grateful afterward.
One of you touches the vein in the other's neck,
Feels the pulse there as a shock, the current of a river
Or the drawing down of milk. Who wants Amida's Western Paradise
When there is all this world for tongue to taste,
Fingers to touch, small hairs like spun silkweed
Furling on another's arms and legs and lower back.
And so you talk. Always then the other shock
Of the singular, lived life, a mother in a rest home,
Maybe, a difficult person, grievous or vindictive.
The gossip of the other servants. A brother who works

As a hosteler at an inn and has grand plans.
You listen. You learned long ago the trick
Of not thinking what you're going to say next
When the other person's speaking. Part of you
Drinks her in like milk. Part of you begins to notice
That she is trying out self-deceptions in the account
Of some difficulty, lazily formulated. You watch her
Shake her head in self-correction; you notice
That she has a mind that wants to get things right.
The tremor of her body makes a nuzzling notion
Along your flank and you reach down to feel again
The wetness which is what we have instead of the luminosity
Of paint. Afterward, in one of those tracks the mind
Returns to when it's on its feet again, she speaks
Of Hans, the butler, how he bullies the girls,
Prays vigorously at hourly intervals on Sunday.
It is Sunday. Now she's getting dressed. You've agreed
To call the cab and take her to her mother
Up in Gronigen. She's grateful, a little teary,
Makes her first small gesture of possession,
Brushing off your coat. Outside you can hear
The hoofbeats of shod horses on the cobbles.
It's the moment when the burden of another person's life
Seems insupportable. We want to be reborn incessantly
But actually doing it begins—have you noticed?
To seem redundant. Here is the life that chose you
And the one you chose. Here is the brush, horsehair,
Hair of the badger, the goat's beard, the sable,
And here is the smell of paint. The volatile, sharp oils
Of linseed, rapeseed. Here is the stench of the essence
Of pinewood in a can of turpentine. Here is the hand,
Flick of wrist, tendon-ripple of the brushstroke. Here—
Cloud, lake water lifting on a summer morning,

Ash and ash and chalky ash—is the stickiness of paint
Adhering to the woven flax of the canvas, here
Is the faithfulness of paint on paint on paint on paint.
Something stays this way we cannot have,
Comes alive because we cannot have it.

DOMESTIC INTERIORS

1.

A house of old, soft, gray, salt-lustered wood,
Windows onto dune grass and a beach.
His wife is upstairs working in her study
When the doorbell rings. The young man at the door,
A Jehovah's Witness, has an Adam's apple
So protuberant it's conducting a flirtation
With deformity. The man, trying not to stare,
Has a saddened panicked premonition
That his wife needs help, and then a stronger feeling
That he has no wife, has never had a wife.
The young man, eyes contracted by concentration,
Is talking about what he calls "the first awakening."

2.

When the lights went out, she drove to town
And bought a lot of candles. The whole village
Was in the general store buying flashlights,
Batteries, oil lamps, oil lamp mantles, fuel,
Telling the story of where they were
When everything went dark, lingering
Awhile in this sudden village in the village.
When she got home, the power was restored.
That's how the radio described it: "power restored."

3.

She woke him to say that everything was loud,
The nightbird's song, the white of the daisies
In the garden in the dark. Then she woke him
To describe headlights on the road across the bay:
They seemed as lonely as the earth. He said
At that hour it must have been a fisherman,
Who was probably baiting line for sand-sharks
As they spoke. He fell asleep imagining
The man setting the line, pouring coffee,
Blowing on his hands, shivering against the cold.
She was awake beside him, her panic like the wind.

4.

It was hot. She was stripping a kitchen chair
She'd bought at a garage sale up the bay.
She was working indoors because the sun
Outside would dry the paint remover
As fast as she applied it. So she worked
In the kitchen, opening the windows
And hoping for a little breeze. Which came and went.
There were three layers of paint on the chair,
She discovered, white, an evergreen shade of green,
Then red, and underneath the paint what looked like cedar.
She scraped hard and watched her mind
Shying from the notion of endeavor.

TWIN DOLPHINS

A paradise of palm and palm and palm
And glittering sea.

Rocks, pelicans, then pure horizon,
Angular white villas on a hillside
Tumbling to the sea.

"Gracias." "De nada."

A flycatcher in an ironwood,
Sulfur belly, whitish throat,
A thin rind of brown-gold on ash-gray wings.
Utterly alert. He has his work to do.

After breakfast they went their separate ways.

Gulls and lulls and glittering sea.

"The papaya was lovely this morning."
"Yes, but the guava was not quite ripe."

Expressionist crucifix: the frigatebird.

Sand-colored day, bright heat.
"What do you call a lot of pelicans?"
"A flotilla." "Ah, a little float."
"A baby fleet." Smell of vanilla
In the desert, and, oddly, maple
(yerba santa?). Making love after,
To the sound of waves,
The sound of waves.

Eden, limbo.

Fan palms and the sea; festoons
Of big-leaved fan palms
Fanning out; the sea on which they pitch
Raking sand and raking sand, sighing
And pitching and raking sand.

Harlequin sparrows in a coral tree.
One halcyon harrying another in the desert sky,
Blue, and would be turquoise,
Would be stone.

Bone china handle of a coffee mug: the moon.

What's old? The silence
In the black, humped porous mass
Of "prefossiliferous rock"
The ocean beats against.

No animals, no plants,
The tides of fire before there was a sea.

Before skin, words.

"Sonorous nutshells rattling vacantly."

Brilliant welter, azure welter,
Occurs—the world occurs—
only in the present tense.

"I'll see you after lunch."
(Kisses him lightly)

"—As if raspberry tanagers in palms,
High up in orange air, were barbarous."

THEN TIME

In winter, in a small room, a man and a woman
Have been making love for hours. Exhausted,
Very busy wringing out each other's bodies,
They look at one another suddenly and laugh.
"What is this?" he says. "I can't get enough of you,"
She says, a woman who thinks of herself as not given
To cliché. She runs her fingers across his chest,
Tentative touches, as if she were testing her wonder.
He says, "Me too." And she, beginning to be herself
Again, "You mean you can't get enough of you either?"
"I mean," he takes her arms in his hands and shakes them,
"Where does this come from?" She cocks her head
And looks into his face. "Do you really want to know?"
"Yes," he says. "Self-hatred," she says, "longing for God."
Kisses him again. "It's not what it is," a wry shrug,
"It's where it comes from." Kisses his bruised mouth
A second time, a third. Years later, in another city,
They're having dinner in a quiet restaurant near a park.
Fall. Earlier that day, hard rain: leaves, brass-colored
And smoky crimson, flying everywhere. Twenty years older,
She is very beautiful. An astringent person. She'd become,
She said, an obsessive gardener, her daughters grown.
He's trying not to be overwhelmed by love or pity
Because he sees she has no hands. He thinks
She must have given them away. He imagines,
Very clearly, how she wakes some mornings
(He has a vivid memory of her younger self, stirred
From sleep, flushed, just opening her eyes)
To momentary horror because she can't remember
What she did with them, why they were gone,
And then remembers, and calms herself, so that the day
Takes on its customary sequence once again.
She asks him if he thinks about her. "Occasionally,"
He says, smiling. "And you?" "Not much," she says,

"I think it's because we never existed inside time."
He studies her long fingers, a pianist's hands,
Or a gardener's, strong, much-used, as she fiddles
With her wineglass and he understands, vaguely,
That it must be his hands that are gone. Then
He's describing a meeting that he'd sat in all day,
Chaired by someone they'd felt, many years before,
Mutually superior to. "You know the expression
'A perfect fool,'" she'd said, and he had liked her tone
Of voice so much. She begins a story of the company
In Maine she orders bulbs from, begun by a Polish refugee
Married to a French-Canadian separatist from Quebec.
It's a story with many surprising turns and a rare
Chocolate-black lily at the end. He's listening,
Studying her face, still turning over her remark.
He decides that she thinks more symbolically
Than he does and that it seemed to have saved her,
For all her fatalism, from certain kinds of pain.
She finds herself thinking what a literal man he is,
Notices, as if she were recalling it, his pleasure
In the menu, and the cooking, and the architecture of the room.
It moves her—in the way that earnest limitation
Can be moving, and she is moved by her attraction to him.
Also by what he was to her. She sees her own avidity
To live then, or not to not have lived might be more accurate,
From a distance, the way a driver might see from the road
A startled deer running across an open field in the rain.
Wild thing. Here and gone. Death made it poignant, or,
If not death exactly, which she'd come to think of
As creatures seething in a compost heap, then time.

THAT MUSIC

The creek's silver in the sun of almost August,
And bright dry air, and last runnels of snowmelt,
Percolating through the roots of mountain grasses
Vinegar weed, golden smoke, or meadow rust,

Do they confer, do the lovers' bodies
In the summer dusk, his breath, her sleeping face,
Confer—, does the slow breeze in the pines?
If you were the interpreter, if that were your task.

In his last years, when he had moved back to Kraków, we worked on the translation of his poems by e-mail and phone. Around the time of his ninetieth birthday, he sent me a set of poems entitled "Oh!" I wrote to ask him if he meant "Oh!" or "O!" and he asked me what the difference was and said that perhaps we should talk on the phone. On the phone I explained that "Oh!" was a long breath of wonder, that the equivalent was, possibly, "Wow!" and that "O!" was a caught breath of wonder and surprise, more like "Huh!" and he said, after a pause, "O! for sure." Here are the translations we made:

O !

I.

O happiness! To see an iris.

The color of indigo, as Ella's dress was once, and the delicate scent was like that of her skin.

O what a mumbling to describe an iris that was blooming when Ella did not exist, nor all our kingdoms, nor all our desmesnes!

2.

GUSTAV KLIMT (1883–1918)
Judith I (detail)
OESTERREICHISCHE GALERIE

O lips half opened, eyes half closed, the rosy nipple of your unveiled
nakedness, Judith!

And they, rushing forward in an attack with your image preserved
in their memories, torn apart by bursts of artillery shells, falling
down into pits, into putrefaction.

O the massive gold of your brocade, of your necklace with its rows of
precious stones, Judith, for such a farewell.

3.

SALVATOR ROSA (1615–1673)
A Landscape with Figures
YALE UNIVERSITY MUSEUM

O the quiet of water under the rocks, and the yellow silence of the
afternoon, and flat white clouds reflected!

Figures in the foreground dressing themselves after bathing, figures
on the other shore tiny, and in their activities mysterious.

O most ordinary, taken from dailiness and elevated to a place like this
earth and not like this earth!

4.

EDWARD HOPPER (1882–1967)
A Hotel Room
THYSSEN-BORNEMISZA COLLECTION, LUGANO

O what sadness unaware that it's sadness!
What despair that doesn't know it's despair!

A business woman, her unpacked suitcase on the floor, sits on a bed
    half undressed, in red underwear, her hair impeccable; she has a
    piece of paper in her hand, probably with numbers.

Who are you? Nobody will ask. She doesn't know either.

HORACE: THREE IMITATIONS

1.

Odes, 1.38   *Persicos odi, puer, apparatus*

I hate Persian filigree, and garlands
Woven out of lime tree bark.
On no account are you to hunt up, for my sake,
    The late-blooming rose.

Plain myrtle will do nicely for a crown.
It's not unbecoming on you as you pour
Or on me as I sip, in the arbor's shade,
    A glass of cool wine.

Here, by the way, is your manumission.
Let it be noted that after two thousand years
The poet Horace, he of the suave Greek meters, has
    At last freed his slaves.

2.

Odes, 3.2   *Angustam amice pauperiem pati*

Let the young, toughened by a soldier's training,
Learn to bear hardship gladly
   And to terrify Parthian insurgents
    From the turrets of their formidable tanks,

Also to walk so easily under desert skies
That the mother of some young Sunni

Will see a marine in the dusty streets
  And turn to the daughter-in-law beside her

And say with a shudder: Pray God our boy
Doesn't stir up that Roman animal
  Whom a cruel rage for blood would drive
    Straight to the middle of any slaughter.

It is sweet, and fit, to die for one's country,
Especially since death doesn't spare deserters
  Or the young man without a warrior's instincts
    Who goes down with a bullet in his back.

Civic courage is a more complicated matter.
Of itself it shines out undefiled.
  It neither lies its way into office, nor mistakes
    The interests of Roman oil for Roman honor.

The kind of courage death can't claim
Doesn't go very far in politics.
  If you are going to speak truth in public places
    You may as well take wing from the earth.

Knowing when not to speak also has its virtue.
I wouldn't sit under the same roof beams
  With most of the explainers of wars on television
    Or set sail on the same sleek ship.

They say the gods have been known
To punish the innocent along with the guilty
  And nemesis often finds the ones it means,
    With its limping gait, to track down.

3.

You talk very well about Inachus
    And how Codrus died for his city,
And the offspring of old Aeacus
    And the fighting at sacred Ilium under the walls,

But on the price of Chian wine,
    And the question of who's going to warm it,
Under whose roof it will be drunk,
    And when my bones will come unfrozen, you are mute.

Boy, let's drink to the new moon's sliver,
    And drink to the middle of the night, and drink
To good Murena, with three glasses
    Or with nine. Nine, says the madman poet

Whom the uneven-numbered Muses love.
    Three, says the even-tempered Grace who holds
Her naked sisters by the hands
    And disapproves altogether of brawling,

Should do a party handsomely.
    But what I want's to rave. Why is the flute
From Phrygia silent? Why are the lyre
    And the reed pipe hanging on the wall?

Oh, how I hate a pinching hand.
    Scatter the roses! Let jealous old Lycus

Listen to our pandemonium,
　　And also the pretty neighbor he's not up to.

Rhoda loves your locks, Telephus.
　　She thinks they glisten like the evening star.
As for me, I'm stuck on Glycera:
　　With a love that smoulders in me like slow fire.

TOMAS TRANSTRÖMER: SONG

Dressed in the ragged sailcloth of dead ships,
Flecked gray with the smokes of outlawed coasts,
The white flock swelled, the swarms of gulls cried out:

Alarm! Alarm! There's something overboard.
They crowded tight to form a signal flag
That, fluttering, reads: Look sharp! There's booty here!

So the gulls steered across the water-widths,
Blue pastures striding in the waves' white foam,
A streak of phosphor straightway to the sun.

But Vainomoinen on his ancient journeys
Sparkles on sea swells in the ancient light,
His horse's hooves so swift they're hardly wet.

And back of him the green forest of his songs:
The oak tree poised to leap a thousand years,
A great mill turned by birdsong, and the wind

Imprisons each of the trees in its own roar.
Immense pinecones glimmer in the moonlight
When the sentinel pine ignites and flares.

It's then the Other rises with his galdar;
The arrow springs from the bow; it sees with song
In the flash of its feathers like a flock of birds.

A dead second when the horse abruptly stiffens,
Then breaks above the gray-blue waterline
Like storm clouds under thunder's quick antennae.

And Vainomoinen heaves into the sea
(A firemen's net the compass points unfurl).
Alarm! Alarm! Gulls swarming where he falls.

So too the man who stands without anxiety,
Bewitched at the center of his fortune's wheel,
With his eleven grain-sheaves gold and bowing

And Trust's alpine heights humming in the ether,
Three thousand meters up where the clouds are holding
A regatta. Sleek, well-fed, the shark wallows

In the waves, silent laughter and an open mouth
(Death and rebirth trade places in the breaking wave)
And the wind cycles peacefully through the leaves.

Drums then, on the horizon, a muffled thunder
(A buffalo herd racing from a prairie fire).
The tree's shadow tightens into a fist

And the man at the center of his fortune's wheel,
Bewitched there, is thrown down. The heavens glow
Behind the wild boar's mask of an evening sky.

His doppelganger has grown envious
And made a secret bargain with his sister.
And the shadow, gathering fast, becomes a wave,

A wave in flood, dark, gulls riding aslant
The foam and the port-heart hissing in the crest.
Death and rebirth trade places in the breaking wave.

Dressed in the ragged sail-cloth of dead ships,
Flecked gray with the signal fires of outlawed coasts,
The white flock swelled, the swarm of gulls cried out.

The gray gull is a velvet-backed harpoon.
Up close, it looks like a snow-covered hull
With a pulse keeping time to a hidden beat.

Its flier's nerves in balance, it lifts and wafts,
It dreams, footloose, hanging in the heavy wind,
Its hunter's dream, its quick, sharpshooter's beak

Plunges, ravenous, toward the surface of the sea
And wriggles around his prey like a gray sock
And tugs and jerks and lifts it like a spirit.

(Rebirth is power's blind métier, a context
More mysterious than the eel's migrations,
An invisible tree blossoming, and as the seal

In its fathoms-deep sleep rises gliding
Toward the ocean's skin and takes a shuddering breath,
Then dives, still sleeping, to the bottom,

So now the Slumberer inside me has,
Secretly, returned, having joined itself to *that*
While I stood with my gaze fastened to something else.)

And the diesel engine throbbing in the swarm
Past the dark skerry, past the bird-infested cliffs
Where hunger's blossoms are the gaping mouths.

You can still hear them as the dark comes on:
Undevelopedness's music, the tentative sounds
The orchestra makes before the piece begins.

But still on his ancient ocean Vainomoinen
Drifted, shaken in the sea's enormous pincers
Or sprawled in the calm's still mirror where the birds

Are magnified. And from a waste seed, very far
From land, at the sea's end, from the heave of waves,
From banks of shrouded sea fogs, it shot up:

An enormous tree with scaly bark and leaves
Utterly transparent, crystalline, and behind them
The billowing sails of distant suns glided

Forward in a trance. And an eagle lifts into the air.

STATE OF THE PLANET

On the occasion of the fiftieth anniversary of the Lamont-Doherty Earth Observatory

I.

October on the planet at the century's end.
Rain lashing the windshield. Through blurred glass
Gusts of a Pacific storm rocking a huge, shank-needled
Himalayan cedar. Under it a Japanese plum
Throws off a vertical cascade of leaves the color
Of skinned copper, if copper could be skinned.
And under it, her gait as elegant and supple
As the young of any of earth's species, a schoolgirl
Negotiates a crosswalk in the wind, her hair flying,
The red satchel on her quite straight back darkening
Splotch by smoky crimson splotch as the rain pelts it.
One of the six billion of her hungry and curious kind.
Inside the backpack, dog-eared, full of illustrations,
A book with a title like *Getting to Know Your Planet*.

The book will tell her that the earth this month
Has yawed a little distance from the sun,
And that the air, cooling, has begun to move,
As sensitive to temperature as skin is
To a lover's touch. It will also tell her that the air—
It's likely to say "the troposphere"—has trapped
Emissions from millions of cars, idling like mine
As she crosses, and is making a greenhouse
Of the atmosphere. The book will say that climate
Is complicated, that we may be doing this,
And if we are, it may explain that this
Was something we've done quite accidentally,
Which she can understand, not having meant
That morning to have spilled the milk. She's
One of those who's only hungry metaphorically.

2.

Poetry should be able to comprehend the earth,
To set aside from time to time its natural idioms
Of ardor and revulsion, and say, in a style as sober
As the Latin of Lucretius, who reported to Venus
On the state of things two thousand years ago—
"It's your doing that under the wheeling constellations
Of the sky," he wrote, "all nature teems with life—"
Something of the earth beyond our human dramas.

Topsoil: going fast. Rivers: dammed and fouled.
Cod: about fished out. Haddock: about fished out.
Pacific salmon nosing against dams from Yokohama
To Kamchatka to Seattle and Portland, flailing
Up fish ladders, against turbines, in a rage to breed
Much older than human beings and interdicted
By the clever means that humans have devised
To grow more corn and commandeer more lights.
Most of the ancient groves are gone, sacred to Kuan Yin
And Artemis, sacred to the gods and goddesses
In every picture book the child is apt to read.

3.

Lucretius, we have grown so clever that mechanics
In our art of natural philosophy can take the property
Of luminescence from a jellyfish and put it in mice.
In the dark the creatures give off greenish light.
Their bodies must be very strange to them.
An artist in Chicago—think of a great trading city
In Dacia or Thracia—has asked to learn the method
So he can sell people dogs that glow in the dark.

4.

The book will try to give the child the wonder
Of how, in our time, we understand life came to be:
Stuff flung off from the sun, the molten core
Still pouring sometimes rivers of black basalt
Across the earth from the old fountains of its origin.
A hundred million years of clouds, sulfurous rain.
The long cooling. There is no silence in the world
Like the silence of rock from before life was.
You come across it in a Mexican desert,

A palo verde tree nearby, moss-green. Some
Insect-eating bird with wing feathers the color
Of a morning sky perched on a limb of the tree.
That blue, that green, the completely fierce
Alertness of the bird that can't know the amazement
Of its being there, a human mind that somewhat does,
Regarding a black outcrop of rock in the desert
Near a sea, charcoal-black and dense, wave-worn,
And all one thing: there's no life in it at all.

It must be a gift of evolution that humans
Can't sustain wonder. We'd never have gotten up
From our knees if we could. But soon enough
We'd have fashioned sexy little earrings from the feathers,
Highlighted our cheekbones by rubbings from the rock,
And made a spear from the sinewey wood of the tree.

5.

If she lived in Michigan or the Ukraine,
She'd find, washed up on the beach in a storm like this
Limestone fossils of Devonian coral. She could study
The faint white markings: she might have to lick the stone
To see them if the wind was drying the pale surface
Even as she held it, to bring back the picture of what life
Looked like four hundred millions years ago: a honeycomb with mouths.

6.

Cells that divided and reproduced. From where? Why?
(In our century it was the fashion in philosophy
Not to ask unanswerable questions. That was left
To priests and poets, an attitude you'd probably
Approve.) Then a bacterium grew green pigment.
This was the essential miracle. It somehow unmated
Carbon dioxide to eat the carbon and turn it
Into sugar and spit out, hiss out the molecules
Of oxygen the child on her way to school
Is breathing, and so bred life. Something then
Of DNA, the curled musical ladder of sugars, acids.
From there to eyes, ears, wings, hands, tongues.
Armadillos, piano tuners, gnats, sonnets,
Military interrogation, the coho salmon, the Margaret Truman rose.

7.

The people who live in Tena, on the Napo River,
Say that the black, viscid stuff that pools in the selva
Is the blood of the rainbow boa curled in the earth's core.

The great trees in that forest house ten thousands of kinds
Of beetle, reptiles no human eyes has ever seen changing
Color on the hot, green, hardly changing leaves
Whenever a faint breeze stirs them. In the understory
Bromeliads and orchids whose flecked petals and womb-
Or mouth-like flowers are the shapes of desire
In human dreams. And butterflies, larger than her palm
Held up to catch a ball or ward off fear. Along the river
Wide-leaved banyans where flocks of raucous parrots,
Fruit-eaters and seed-eaters, rise in startled flares
Of red and yellow and bright green. It will seem to be poetry
Forgetting its promise of sobriety to say the rosy shinings
In the thick brown current are small dolphins rising
To the surface where gouts of the oil that burns inside
The engine of the car I'm driving oozes from the banks.

8.

The book will tell her that the gleaming appliance
That kept her milk cold in the night required
Chlorofluorocarbons—Lucretius, your master
Epictetus was right about atoms in a general way.
It turns out they are electricity having sex
In an infinite variety of permutations, Plato's
Yearning halves of a severed being multiplied
In all the ways that all the shapes on earth
Are multiple, complex; the philosopher
Who said that the world was fire was also right—
Chlorofluorocarbons react with ozone, the gas
That makes air tingle on a sparkling day.
Nor were you wrong to describe them as assemblies,
As if evolution were a town meeting or a plebiscite.
(Your theory of wind, and of gases, was also right

And there are more of them than you supposed.)
Ozone, high in the air, makes a kind of filter
Keeping out parts of sunlight damaging to skin.
The device we use to keep our food as cool
As if it sat in snow required this substance,
And it reacts with ozone. Where oxygen breeds it
From ultra-violet light, it burns a hole in the air.

9.

They drained the marshes around Rome. Your people,
You know, were the ones who taught the world to love
Vast fields of grain, the power and the order of the green,
Then golden rows of it, spooled out almost endlessly.
Your poets, those in the generation after you,
Were the ones who praised the packed seed heads
And the vineyards and the olive groves and called them
"Smiling" fields. In the years since, we've gotten
Even better at relentless simplification, but it's taken
Until our time for it to crowd out, savagely, the rest
Of life. No use to rail against our curiosity and greed.
They keep us awake. And are, for all their fury
And their urgency, compatible with intelligent restraint.
In the old paintings of the Italian renaissance,
—In the fresco painters who came after you
(It was the time in which your poems were rediscovered—
There was a period when you, and Venus, were lost;
How could she be lost? you may well ask). Anyway
In those years the painters made of our desire
An allegory and a dance in the figure of three graces.
The first, the woman coming toward you, is the appetite
For life; the one who seems to turn away is chaste restraint,

And the one whom you've just glimpsed, her back to you,
Is beauty. The dance resembles wheeling constellations.
They made of it a figure for something elegant or lovely
Forethought gives our species. One would like to think
It makes a dance; that the black-and-white flash
Of a flock of buntings in October wind, headed south
Toward winter habitat, would find that the December fields
Their kind has known and mated in for thirty centuries
Or more, were still intact, that they will not go
The way of the long-billed arctic curlews who flew
From Newfoundland to Patagonia in every weather
And are gone now from the kinds on earth. The last of them
Seen by any human alit in a Texas marsh in 1964.

10.

What is to be done with our species? Because
We know we're going to die, to be submitted
To that tingling dance of atoms once again,
It's easy for us to feel that our lives are a dream—
As this is, in a way, a dream: the flailing rain,
The birds, the soaked red backpack of the child,
Her tendrils of wet hair, the windshield wipers,
This voice trying to speak across the centuries
Between us, even the long story of the earth,
Boreal forests, mangrove swamps, Tiberian wheatfields
In the summer heat on hillsides south of Rome—all of it
A dream, and we alive somewhere, somehow outside it,
Watching. People have been arguing for centuries
About whether or not you thought of Venus as a metaphor.
Because of the rational man they take you for.
Also about why your poem ended with a plague,

The bodies heaped in the temple of the gods.
To disappear. First one, then a few, then hundreds,
Just stopping over here, to vanish in the marsh at dusk.
So easy, in imagination, to tell the story backward,
Because the earth needs a dream of restoration—
She dances and the birds just keep arriving,
Thousands of them, immense arctic flocks, her teeming life.

POEM WITH A CUCUMBER IN IT

Sometimes from this hillside just after sunset
The rim of the sky takes on a tinge
Of the palest green, like the flesh of a cucumber
When you peel it carefully.

*

In Crete once, in the summer,
When it was still hot at midnight,
We sat in a taverna by the water
Watching the squid boats rocking in the moonlight,
Drinking retsina and eating salads
Of cool, chopped cucumber and yogurt and a little dill.

*

A hint of salt, something like starch, something
Like an attar of grasses or green leaves
On the tongue is the tongue
And the cucumber
Evolving toward each other.

*

Since *cumbersome* is a word,
Cumber must have been a word,
Lost to us now, and even then,
For a person feeling encumbered,
It must have felt orderly and right-minded
To stand at a sink and slice a cucumber.

*

If you think I am going to make
A sexual joke in this poem, you are mistaken.

*

In the old torment of the earth
When the fires were cooling and disposing themselves
Into granite and limestone and serpentine and shale,
It is possible to imagine that, under yellowish chemical clouds,
The molten froth, having burned long enough,
Was already dreaming of release,
And that the dream, dimly
But with increasingly distinctness, took the form
Of water, and that it was then, still more dimly, that it imagined
The dark green skin and opal green flesh of cucumbers.

DRIFT AND VAPOR (SURF FAINTLY)

How much damage do you think we do,
making love this way when we can hardly stand
each other?—I can stand you. You're the rare person
I can always stand.—Well, yes, but you know what I mean.
—I'm not sure I do. I think I'm more light-hearted
about sex than you are. I think it's a little tiresome
to treat it like a fucking sacrament.—Not much of a pun.
—Not much. (She licks tiny wavelets of dried salt
from the soft flesh of his inner arm. He reaches up
to whisk sand from her breast.)—And I do like you. Mostly.
I don't think you can expect anyone's imagination
to light up over the same person all the time. (Sand,
peppery flecks of it, cling to the rosy, puckered skin
of her aureola in the cooling air. He studies it,
squinting, then sucks her nipple lightly.)—Umnh.
—I'm angry. You're not really here. We come
as if we were opening a wound.—Speak for yourself.
(A young woman, wearing the ochre apron of the hotel staff,
emerges from dune grass in the distance. She carries
snow-white towels they watch her stack on a table
under an umbrella made of palm fronds.)—Look,
I know you're hurt. I think you want me
to feel guilty and I don't.—I don't want you
to feel guilty.—What do you want then?
—I don't know. Dinner. (The woman is humming something
they hear snatches of, rising and fading on the breeze.)
—That's the girl who lost her child last winter.
—How do you know these things? (She slips
Into her suit top.)—I talk to people. I talked
To the girl who cleans our room. (He squints
Down the beach again, shakes his head.)
—Poor kid. (She kisses his cheekbone.
He squirms into his trunks.)

". . . WHITE OF FORGETFULNESS, WHITE OF SAFETY"

My mother was burning in a closet.

Creek water wrinkling over stones.

Sister Damien, in fifth grade, loved teaching mathematics.
Her full white sleeve, when she wrote on the board,
Swayed like the slow movement of a hunting bird,
Egret in the tidal flats,
Swan paddling in a pond.

Let A equal the distance between x and y.

The doves in the desert,
Their cinnamon coverts when they flew.

People made arguments. They had reasons for their appetites.
A child could see it wasn't true.

In the picture of the Last Supper on the classroom wall,
All the apostles had beautiful pastel robes,
Each one the color of a flavor of sherbet.

A line is the distance between two points.

A point is indivisible.

Not a statement of fact; a definition.

It took you a second to understand the difference,
And then you loved it, loved reason,
Moving as a swan moves in a mill stream.

I would not have betrayed the Lord
Before the cock crowed thrice,
But I was a child, what could I do
When they came for him?

Ticking heat, the scent of sage,
Of pennyroyal. The structure of every living thing
Was praying for rain.

AFTER GOETHE

In all the mountains,
Stillness;
In the treetops
Not a breath of wind.
The birds are silent in the woods.
Just wait: soon enough
You will be quiet too.

I AM YOUR WAITER TONIGHT
AND MY NAME IS DMITRI

Is, more or less, the title of a poem by John Ashbery and has
No investment in the fact that you can get an adolescent
Of the human species to do almost anything (and when adolescence
In the human species ends is what The Fat Man in *The Maltese Falcon*
Calls "a nice question, sir, a very nice question indeed")
Which is why they are tromping down a road in Fallujah
In combat gear and a hundred and fifteen degrees of heat
This morning and why a young woman is strapping
Twenty pounds of explosives to her mortal body in Jerusalem.
Dulce et decorum est pro patria mori. Have I mentioned
That the other law of human nature is that human beings
Will do anything they see someone else do and someone
Will do almost anything? There is probably a waiter
In this country so clueless he wears a T-shirt in the gym
That says Da Meat Tree. Not our protagonist. American amnesia
Is such that he may very well be the great-grandson
Of the elder Karamazov brother who fled to the Middle West
With his girl friend Grushenka—he never killed his father,
It isn't true that he killed his father—but his religion
Was that woman's honey-colored head, an ideal tangible
Enough to die for, and he lived for it: in Buffalo,
New York, or Sandusky, Ohio. He never learned much English,
But he slept beside her in the night until she was an old woman
Who still knew her way to the Russian pharmacist
In a Chicago suburb where she could buy sachets of the herbs
Of the Russian summer that her coarse white nightgown
Smelled of as he fell asleep, though he smoked Turkish cigarettes
And could hardly smell. Grushenka got two boys out of her body,
One was born in 1894, the other in 1896,
The elder having died in the mud at the Battle of the Somme
From a piece of shrapnel manufactured by Alfred Nobel.
Metal traveling at that speed works amazing transformations

On the tissues of the human intestine; the other son worked
    construction
The year his mother died. If they could have, they would have,
If not filled, half-filled her coffin with the petals
Of buckwheat flowers from which Crimean bees made the honey
Bought in the honey market in St. Petersburg (not far
From the place where Raskolnikov, himself an adolescent male,
Couldn't kill the old moneylender without killing her saintly sister,
But killed her nevertheless in a fit of guilt and reasoning
Which went something like this: since the world
Evidently consists in the ravenous pursuit of wealth
And power and in the exploitation and prostitution
Of women, except the wholly self-sacrificing ones
Who make you crazy with guilt, and since I am going
To be the world, I might as well take an axe to the head
Of this woman who symbolizes both usury and the guilt
The virtue and suffering of women induces in men,
And be done with it). I frankly admit the syntax
Of that sentence, like the intestines slithering from the hands
Of the startled boys clutching their belly wounds
At the Somme, has escaped my grip. I step over it
Gingerly. Where were we? Not far from the honey market,
Which is not far from the hay market. It is important
To remember that the teeming cities of the nineteenth century
Were site central for horsewhipping. Humans had domesticated
The race of horses five thousand years before, harnessed them,
Trained them, whipped them mercilessly for recalcitrance
In Vienna, Prague, Naples, London, and Chicago, according
To the novels of the period which may have been noticing this
For the first time or registering an actual statistical increase
In either human brutality or the insurrectionary impulse
In horses, which were fed hay, so there was, of course,
In every European city a hay market like the one in which

Raskolnikov kissed the earth from a longing for salvation.
Grushenka, though Dostoyevsky made her, probably did not
Have much use for novels of ideas. Her younger son,
A master carpenter, eventually took a degree in engineering
From Bucknell University. He married an Irish girl
From Vermont who was descended from the gardener
Of Emily Dickinson, but that's another story. Their son
In Iwo Jima died. Gangrene. But he left behind, curled
In the body of the daughter of a Russian Jewish cigar maker
From Minsk, the fetal curl of a being who became the lead dancer
In the Cleveland Ballet, radiant Tanya, who turned in
A bad knee sometime early 1971, just after her brother ate it
In Cao Dai Dien, for marriage and motherhood, which brings us
To our waiter, Dmitri, who, you will have noticed, is not in Bagdad.
He doesn't even want to be an actor. He has been offered
Roles in several major motion pictures and refused them
Because he is, in fact, under contract to John Ashbery
Who is a sane and humane man and has no intention
Of releasing him from the poem. You can get killed out there.
He is allowed to go home for his mother's birthday and she
Has described to him on the phone—a cell phone, he's
Walking down Christopher Street with such easy bearing
He could be St. Christopher bearing innocence across a river—
Having come across a lock, the delicate curl of a honey-
Colored lock of his great-grandmother's Crimean-
Honey-bee-pollen, Russian-spring-wildflower-sachet-
Scented hair in the attic, where it released for her
In the July heat and raftery midsummer dark the memory
Of an odor like life itself carried to her on the wind.
Here is your sea bass with a light lemon and caper sauce.
Here is your dish of raspberries and chocolate; notice
Their subtle transfiguration of the colors of excrement and blood;
And here are the flecks of crystallized lavender that stipple it.

A POEM

"You would think God would relent," the American poet Richard
Eberhardt wrote during World War II, "listening to the fury of
aerial bombardment." Of course, God is not the cause of aerial
bombardment. During the Vietnam War, the United States hired the
RAND Corporation to conduct a study of the effects in the peasant
villages of Vietnam of their policy of saturation bombing of the
countryside. That policy had at least two purposes: to defoliate the
tropical forests as a way of locating the enemy and to kill the enemy if
he happened to be in the way of the concussion bombs or the napalm
or the firebombs. The RAND Corporation sent a young scholar
named Leon Goure to Vietnam. His study was rushed by the air force
which was impatient for results, but he was able to conduct interviews
through interpreters with farmers in the Mekong Delta and the
mountainous hillside farm regions around Hue. He concluded that
the incidental damage to civilian lives was very considerable and that
the villagers were angry and afraid, but he also found that they blamed
the Viet Cong—the insurrectionist army the U.S. was fighting—and
not the United States for their troubles, because they thought of the
Viet Cong as their legitimate government and felt it wasn't protecting
them. Seeing that the bombing was alienating the peasantry from
the enemy Vietnamese, Robert McNamara, the secretary of defense,
General William Westmoreland, the commander in charge of
prosecuting the war, and Lyndon Johnson, the president of the
United States, ordered an intensification of the bombing. In the end,
there were more bombs dropped on the villages and forests of South
Vietnam than were dropped in all of World War II. The estimated
Vietnamese casualties during the war is two million. It was a war whose
principle strategy was terror. More Iraqi civilians have now been
incidental casualties of the conduct of the war in Iraq than were killed
by Arab terrorists in the destruction of the World Trade Center.
In the first twenty years of the twentieth century 90 percent of war
deaths were the deaths of combatants. In the last twenty years of the
twentieth century 90 percent of war deaths were deaths of civilians.

There are imaginable responses to these facts. The nations of the world could stop setting an example for suicide bombers. They could abolish the use of land mines. They could abolish the use of aerial bombardment in warfare. You would think men would relent.

I typed the brief phrase, "Bush's War,"
At the top of a sheet of white paper,
Having some dim intuition of a poem
Made luminous by reason that would,
Though I did not have them at hand,
Set the facts out in an orderly way.
Berlin is a northerly city. In May
At the end of the twentieth century
In the leafy precincts of Dahlem Dorf,
South of the Grunewald, near Krumme Lanke,
The northern spring begins before dawn
In a racket of birdsong, when the *amsels,*
Black European thrushes, shiver the sun up
As if they were shaking a great tangle
Of golden wire. There are two kinds
Of flowering chestnuts, red and white,
And the wet pavements are speckled
With petals from the incandescent spikes
Of their flowers; the shoes at U-Bahn stops
Are flecked with them. Green of holm oaks,
Birch tassels, the soft green of maples,
And the odor of lilacs is everywhere.
At Oskar-Helene-Heim station a farmer
Sells white asparagus from a heaped table.
In a month he'll be selling chanterelles;
In the month after that, strawberries
And small, rosy crawfish from the Spree.
The piles of stalks of the asparagus
Are startlingly phallic, phallic and tender
And deathly pale. Their seasonal appearance
Must be the remnant of some fertility ritual
Of the German tribes. Steamed, they are the color
Of old ivory. In May, in restaurants

They are served on heaped white platters
With boiled potatoes and parsley butter,
Or shavings of Parma ham and lemon juice
Or sprigs of sorrel and smoked salmon. And,
Walking home in the slant, widening,
Brilliant northern light that falls
On the new-leaved birches and the elms,
Nightingales singing at the first, subtlest,
Darkening of dusk, it is a trick of the mind
That the past seems just ahead of us,
As if we were being shunted there
In the surge of a rattling funicular.
Flash forward: firebombing of Hamburg,
Fifty thousand dead in a single night,
"The children's bodies the next day
Set in the street in rows like a market
In charred chicken." Flash forward:
Firebombing of Tokyo, a hundred thousand
In a night. Flash forward: forty-five
Thousand Polish officers slaughtered
By the Russian army in the Katyn Woods,
The work of half a day. Flash forward:
Two million Russian prisoners of war
Murdered by the German army all across
The eastern front, supplies low,
Winter of 1943. Flash: Hiroshima.
Flash: Auschwitz, Dachau, Thersienstadt,
The train lurching and the stomach woozy
Past the displays of falls of hair, the piles
Of monogrammed valises, spectacles. Flash:
The gulags, seven million in Byelorussia
And Ukraine. In innocent Europe on a night
In spring, among the light-struck birches,

Students holding hands. One of them
Is carrying a novel, the German translation
Of a slim book by Marguerite Duras
About a love affair in old Saigon. (Flash:
Two million Vietnamese, fifty-five thousand
Of the American young, whole races
Of tropical birds extinct from saturation bombing)
The kind of book the young love
To love, about love in time of war.
Forty-five million, all told, in World War II.
In Berlin, pretty Berlin, in the springtime,
You are never not wondering how
It happened, and these Germans, too,
Children then, or unborn, never not
Wondering. Is it that we like the kissing
And bombing together, in prospect
At least, girls in their flowery dresses?
Someone will always want to mobilize
Death on a massive scale for economic
Domination or revenge. And the task, taken
As a task, appeals to the imagination.
The military is an engineering profession.
Look at boys playing: they love
To figure out the ways to blow things up.
But the rest of us have to go along.
Why do we do it? Certainly there's a rage
To injure what's injured us. Wars
Are always pitched to us that way.
The well-paid news readers read the reasons
On the air. And the us who are injured,
Or have been convinced that we are injured,
Are always identified with virtue. It's
That—the rage to hurt mixed up

With self-righteousness—that's murderous.
The young Arab depiliated himself as an act
Of purification before he drove the plane
Into the office building. It's not just
The violence, it's a taste for power
That amounts to contempt for the body.
The rest of us have to act like we believe
The dead women in the rubble of Baghdad
Who did not cast a vote for their deaths
Or the raw white of the exposed bones
In the bodies of their men or their children
Are being given the gift of freedom
Which is the virtue of the injured us.
It's hard to say which is worse, the moral
Sloth of it or the intellectual disgrace.
And what good is indignation to the dead?
Or our mild forms of rational resistance?
And death the cleanser, Walt Whitman's
Sweet death, the scourer, the tender
Lover, shutter of eyelids, turns
The heaped bodies into summer fruit,
Magpies eating dark berries in the dusk
And birch pollen staining sidewalks
To the faintest gold. *Bald nur*—Goethe—no,
Warte nur, bald ruhest du auch. Just wait.
You will be quiet soon enough. In Dahlem,
under the chestnuts, in the leafy spring.

PEARS

My English uncle, a tall, shambling man, is very old
In the dream (he has been dead for thirty years)
And wears his hound's-tooth jacket of soft tweed.
Standing against one wall, he looks nervous, panicked.
When I walk up to him to ask if he is all right, he explains
In his wry way that he is in the midst of an anxiety attack
Which has immobilized him. He can't move. "Fault
Of Arthur Conan Doyle." I remembered the story.
He was raised among almond orchards on a ranch
In the dry hot California foothills. Something
About reading a description of an illness—
Scarlet fever, I think (in the dream it was scarlet fever)—
And the illustration of a dying child, "the dew of death"
Spotting her forehead in the Edwardian woodcut—
Reading by oil lamp a book that his parents had brought
From Liverpool, the deep rural dark outside of winter
And night and night sounds at the turn of the last century—
He had cried out and hurled the book across the room.
He had told this story in an amused drawl (but not
In the dream, in my memory of a childhood summer
Which was not a dream, may not have been a dream)
In a canoe on the river, paddle in his hand, eyes
Looking past us at the current and the green surface
Of the water. "Agggh." He had imitated the sound—
I must have been six, the story not addressed to me—
And made a gesture of hurling with the stem of the paddle.
In the dream something had triggered this memory
And the paralyzing fear. I ask him how I can help.
"Just don't go away," he says, calling me "young Robert,"
As he did, as I remember he did. He takes my hand
And his helplessness in my dream—he was
The most competent of men, had served in the infantry
At Meuse-Argonne—brings me, in the dream,

To tears. There is a view onto a garden from the upper room
Where he stands with his back pinned to the wall.
He has begun to weep, his shoulders shaking.
Now, outside the dream, I remember overhearing
Him describe the battle of—was it Belleau Wood?—
The Argonne forest??—as a butcher shop, also in his wry,
Slightly barking voice, and then he put down a card,
My parents and my aunt and he played bridge—
And said, "A very smoky butcher shop." Now,
Not in the dream, an image of the small cut glass dish
Into which my aunt put the small festively colored candies
That were called "a bridge mix." And the memory
Of a taste like anise, like a California summer.
Though I don't know how I know it, I know
That there had been a long and lavish party
On the lawn outside which resembles, oddly,
The Luxembourg Gardens and, somewhere
In the dream, I notice, to my surprise, a bird,
Brilliantly yellow, a European goldfinch, perhaps,
Red in the wingtips, high up among the leaves
Of an espaliered pear tree, on which each of the pears
Has been wrapped in a translucent paper packet.
I experience my interest in the bird as irresponsible.
My uncle is holding my hand very tightly and I am
Leaning just a little to the left to see the bird more clearly—
I think it is red on the wingtips—and from that angle
I can see the child's body slumped under the pear tree,
And think, "Well, that explains his panic," and,
When I look again, the bird, of course, has flown.

Our Grandma Dahling arrived from the train station
In a limousine: an old Lincoln touring car
With immense, black, shiny, rounded fenders
And a silver ornament of Nike on the hood.
She wore a long black coat and pearl-gray gloves.
White hair, very soft white, and carefully curled.
Also rimless glasses with thin gold frames.
Once in the house, having presented ourselves
To be hugged completely, the important thing
Was to watch her take off her large, black,
Squarish, thatched, and feathered confection of a hat.
She raised both hands above her head, elbows akimbo,
Lifting the black scrim of a veil in the process,
Removed a pin from either side, and lifted it,
Gingerly, straight up, as if it were a saucer of water
That I must not spill, and then she set it down,
Carefully, solicitously even, as if it were a nest
Of fledgling birds (which it somewhat resembled),
And then there arrived, after she had looked at the hat
For a moment to see that it wasn't going to move,
The important thing. Well, she would say, well, now,
In a musical German-inflected English, touching together
Her two soft, white, ungloved hands from which emanated
The slightly spiced, floral scent of some hand lotion
That made the hands of great-grandmothers singularly soft,
And regard us, and shake her head just a little, but for a while,
To express her wonder at our palpable bodies before her,
And then turn to her suitcase on the sea chest in the hall,
Not having been transferred yet to her bedroom by my father
Who had hauled it up the long, precipitous front stairs;
She flipped open the brass clasps and the shield-shaped lock
She had not locked and opened the case to a lavender interior
From which rose the scent of chocolate, mingled faintly

With the smell of anise from the Christmas cookies
That she always baked. But first were the paper mats
From the dining car of the California Zephyr, adorned
With soft pastel images of what you might see
From the Vista Car: Grand Canyon, Mount Shasta,
A slightly wrinkled Bridal Veil Falls, and, serene, contemplative
Almost, a view of Lake Louise, intimate to me because,
Although it was Canadian, it bore my mother's name.
My brother and I each got two views. He, being the eldest,
Always took Grand Canyon, which I found obscurely terrifying
And so being second was always a relief. I took Lake Louise
And he took Half Dome and the waterfall, and she looked surprised
That we were down to one and handed me the brooding angel,
Shasta. And then from under layers of shimmery print dresses,
She produced, as if relieved that it wasn't lost, the largest chocolate
    bar
That either of us had ever seen. Wrapped in dignified brown paper,
On which ceremonial, silvery capital letters must have announced—
I couldn't read—the sort of thing it was. These were the war years.
Chocolate was rationed. The winey, dark scent rose like manna
In the air and filled the room. My brother, four years older,
Says this never happened. Not once. She never visited the house
On Jackson Street with its sea air and the sound of fog horns
At the Gate. I thought it might help to write it down here
That the truth of things might be easier to come to
On a quiet evening in the clear, dry, mountain air.

The white water rush of some warbler's song.
Last night, a few strewings of ransacked moonlight
On the sheets. You don't know what slumped forward
In the nineteen-forties taxi or why they blamed you
Or what the altered landscape, willowy, riparian,
Had to do with the reasons why everyone
Should be giving things away, quickly,
Except for spendthrift sorrow that can't bear
The need to be forgiven and keeps looking for something
To forgive. The motion of washing machines
Is called agitation. Object constancy is a term
Devised to indicate what a child requires
From days. Clean sheets are an example
Of something that, under many circumstances,
A person can control. The patterns moonlight makes
Are chancier, and dreams, well, dreams
Will have their way with you, their way
With you, will have their way.

POET'S WORK

1.

You carry a saucer of clear water,
Smelling faintly of lemon, that spills
Into the dark roots of what
Was I saying? Hurt or dance, the stunned
Hours, arguments for and against:
There's a tap here somewhere.

2.

This dream: on white linen, in the high ceilinged room,
Marie and Julia had spread baskets of focaccia,
A steaming zucchini torte, ham in thin, almost deliquescent slices,
Mottled ovals of salami, around a huge bowl in which chunks of
    crabmeat,
With its sweet, iodine smell of high tide, were strewn
Among quarter moons of sun-colored tomatoes and lettuce leaves
Of some species as tender-looking as the child's death had been.

3.

If there is a way in, it may be
Through the corolla of the cinquefoil
With its pale yellow petals,
In the mixed smell of dust and water
At trailside in the middle reaches of July.
Soft: an almost phospher gleam in twilight.

MOUTH SLIGHTLY OPEN

The body a yellow brilliance and a head
Some orange color from a Chinese painting
Dipped in sunset by the summer gods
Who are also producing that twitchy shiver
In the cottonwoods, less wind than river,
Where the bird you thought you saw
Was, whether you believe what you thought
You saw or not, and then was not, had
Absconded, leaving behind the emptiness
That hums a little in you now, and is not bad
Or sad, and only just resembles awe or fear.
The bird is elsewhere now, and you are here.

OLD MOVIE WITH THE SOUND
TURNED OFF

The hatcheck girl wears a gown that glows;
The cigarette girl in the black fishnet stockings
And a skirt of black, gauzy, bunched-up tulle
That bobs above the pert muffin of her bottom—
She must be twenty-two—would look like a dancer
In Degas except for the tray of cigarettes that rests
Against her—*tummy* might have been the decade's word,
And the thin black strap which binds it to her neck
And makes the whiteness of her skin seem swan's-down
White. Some quality in the film stock that they used
Made everything so shiny that the films could not
Not make the whole world look like lingerie, like
Phosphorescent milk with winking shadows in it.
All over the world the working poor put down their coins,
Poured into theaters on Friday nights. The manager raffled—
"Raffled off," we used to say in San Rafael in my postwar
Childhood into which the custom had persisted—
Sets of dishes in the intermission of the double feature—
Of the kind they called Fiestaware. And now
The gangster has come in, surrounded by an entourage
Of prize fighters and character actors, all in tuxedo
And black overcoats—except for him. His coat is camel
(Was it the material or the color?—my mind wanders
To earth-colored villages in Samara or Afghanistan).
He is also wearing a white scarf which seems to shimmer
As he takes it off, after he takes off the gray fedora
And hands it to the hatcheck girl. The singer,
In a gown of black taffeta that throws off light
In starbursts, wears black gloves to her elbows
And as she sings, you sense she is afraid.
Not only have I seen this film before—the singer
Shoots the gangster just when he thinks he's been delivered
From a nemesis involving his brother, the district attorney,

And a rival mob—I know the grandson of the cigarette girl,
Who became a screenwriter and was blackballed later
Because she raised money for the Spanish Civil War.
Or at least that's the story as I remember it, so that,
When the gangster is clutching his wounded gut
And delivering a last soundless quip and his scarf
Is still looking like the linen in Heaven, I realize
That it is for them a working day and that the dead
Will rise uncorrupted and change into flannel slacks,
Hawaiian shirts; the women will put on summer smocks
Made from the material superior dish towels are made of
Now, and they'll all drive up to Malibu for drinks.
All the dead actors were pretty in their day. Why
Am I watching this movie? you may ask. Well, my beloved,
Down the hall, is probably laboring over a poem
And is not to be disturbed. And look! I have rediscovered
The sweetness and the immortality of art. The actress
Wrote under a pseudonym, died, I think, of cancer of the lungs.
So many of them did. Far better for me to be doing this
(A last lurid patch of fog out of which the phrase "The End"
Comes swimming; the music I can't hear surging now
Like fate) than reading with actual attention my field guides
Which inform me that the flower of the incense cedar
I saw this morning by the creek is "unisexual, solitary, and terminal."

EZRA POUND'S PROPOSITION

Beauty is sexual, and sexuality
Is the fertility of the earth and the fertility
Of the earth is economics. Though he is no recommendation
For poets on the subject of finance,
I thought of him in the thick heat
Of the Bangkok night. Not more than fourteen, she saunters up to
     you
Outside the Shangri-la Hotel
And says, in plausible English,
"How about a party, big guy?"

Here is more or less how it works:
The World Bank arranges the credit and the dam
Floods three hundred villages, and the villagers find their way
To the city where their daughters melt into the teeming streets,
And the dam's great turbines, beautifully tooled
In Lund or Dresden or Detroit, financed
By Lazard Frères in Paris or the Morgan Bank in New York,
Enabled by judicious gifts from Bechtel of San Francisco
Or Halliburton of Houston to the local political elite,
Spun by the force of rushing water,
Have become hives of shimmering silver
And, down river, they throw that bluish throb of light
Across her cheekbones and her lovely skin.

ON VISITING THE DMZ AT PANMUNJOM: A HAIBUN

The human imagination does not do very well with large numbers.
More than two and a half million people died during the Korean
War. It seems that it ought to have taken more time to wreck so many
bodies. Five hundred thousand Chinese soldiers died in battle, or of
disease. A million South Koreans died, four-fifths of them civilians.
One million, one hundred thousand North Koreans. The terms are
inexact and thinking about them can make you sleepy. Not all "South
Koreans" were born in the south of Korea; some were born in the
north and went south, for reasons of family, or religion, or politics,
at the time of the division of the country. Likewise the "North
Koreans." During the war one half of all the houses in the country
were destroyed and almost all industrial and public buildings.
Pyongyang was bombarded with one thousand bombs per square
kilometer in a city that had been the home to four hundred thousand
people. Twenty-six thousand American soldiers died in the war.
There is no evidence that human beings have absorbed these facts,
which ought, at least, to provoke some communal sense of shame. It
may be the sheer number of bodies that is hard to hold in mind. That
is perhaps why I felt a slight onset of nausea as we were moved from
the civilian bus to the military bus at Panmunjom. The young soldiers
had been trained to do their jobs and they carried out the transfer
of our bodies, dressed for summer in the May heat, with a precision
and dispatch that seemed slightly theatrical. They were young men.
They wanted to be admired. I found it very hard to describe to
myself what I felt about them, whom we had made our instrument.

The flurry of white between the guard towers
    —river mist? a wedding party?
is cattle egrets nesting in the willows.

CONSCIOUSNESS

First image is blue sky, nothing in it, and not
understood as sky, a field of blue.

The second image is auditory: the moan of a foghorn.

We had been arguing about the nature of
consciousness, or avoiding arguing, talking.

Dean had read a book that said that consciousness was like a
knock-knock joke, some notion of an answering call having
brought it into being which was, finally, itself anticipating
an answer from itself, echo of an echo of an echo.

My mind went seven places at once.

One place was a line of ridge somewhere in a dry Western landscape
just after sundown, I saw a pair of coyotes appear suddenly on the
ridge edge and come to a loping stop and sniff the air and look down
toward a valley in the moonlight, tongues out in that way that looks
to us like happiness, though it isn't necessarily; I suppose they were
an idea of mammal consciousness come over the event horizon in
some pure form, hunter-attention, life-in-the-body attention.

CD said human consciousness shows up in the
record as symbolic behavior toward the dead.

My mind also went to Whitman, not interested, he said, in
the people who need to say that we all die and life is a suck
and a sell and two plus two is four and nothing left over.

I think I respond with such quick hostility to anything that smells
like reductionist materialism because it was my father's worldview.

"Bobby," he was sitting in a chair on the porch of the old house on D Street, "it's a dog-eat-dog world out there." I was drawing with crayons on the stairs. Across the street the Haleys' collie Butch was humping the McLaughlins' collie Amanda on the Mullens' front lawn, their coats shuddering like a wheat field in August.

Those stairs: there were five of them. I took three in a
leap, coming home from school, and then four, and
one day five, and have complicated feelings about the
fact that it was one of the vivid pleasures of my life.

When I came into the room where he was dying of cancer, my father gave me a look that was pure plea and I felt a flaring of anger. What was I supposed to do? He was supposed to teach me how to die.

And a few minutes later when he was dead, I felt such a mix of
love and anger and dismay and relief at the sudden peacefulness
of his face that I wanted to whack him on the head with his
polished walnut walking stick which was standing against
the wall in a corner like the still mobile part of him.

My mind also went to Paris, steam on summer mornings rising
off the streets the municipal workers had watered down at the
corner of rue de l'Ecole de Médecin and rue Dupuytren, I suppose
because that city is a product, among other things, of human
consciousness, and whatever else it is, it isn't a knock-knock joke.

My grandmother used to say what a good baby I was, that
they would put me in a crib on the roof of the house on
Jackson Street in the sunlight and the smell of sea air from
the Golden Gate and that I never cried; they'd check to see
if I was sleeping and I wasn't; my eyes would be wide open,
I seemed to be content to lie there looking at the sky.

So I think that first image of consciousness in my consciousness
is not the memory of a visual perception but the invention of the
image of a visual perception—the picture of a field of pure blue—that
came into my head when my grandmother told me that story.

Outside the sound of summer construction starting up. From
my window I see a chickaree come out of the dry grasses, pale
gold in the early morning light, and raise little puffs of dust as
it bounds across the road, going somewhere, going about its
chickaree business, which at this season must be mostly provision.

It was years before I understood that my father was telling his
young son that he hated the job he had to go to every day.

It's hard to see what you're seeing with, to see what being is as an
activity through the instrument of whatever-it-is we have being in.

Consciousness, "that means nothing," Czesław wrote. "That loves
itself," George Oppen wrote. My poor father.

EXIT, PURSUED BY A SIERRA MEADOW

That slow, rhythmic flickering of wings,
As if from the ache of pleasure—
A California tortoiseshell
Hovering over a few white milkweeds.

Smell of water in the dry air,
The almost nutmeg smell of dust.

Good-bye, white fir, Jeffrey pine.
I have no way of knowing whether you prefer
Summer or winter,
Though I think you are more beautiful in winter.

Scarlet gilia, corn lily,
I don't know which you prefer, either.
So long, horse mint,
Your piebald mix of lavender and soft gray-green under the
    cottonwoods
On a shelf of lichened granite near a creek
May be the most startling thing in these mountains,
Besides the mountains.
It's good that we stopped just a minute
To look at you and then walked down the trail
Because we had things to do
And because beauty is a little unendurable,
I mean, getting used to it is unendurable,
Because if we can't eat a thing or do something with it,
Human beings get bored by almost everything eventually,
Which is why winter is such an admirable invention.
There's another month of summer here.
August will squeeze the sweetness out of you
And drift it as pollen.

SEPTEMBER, INVERNESS

Tomales Bay is flat blue in the Indian summer heat.
This is the time when hikers on Inverness Ridge
Stand on tiptoe to pick ripe huckleberries
That the deer can't reach. This is the season of lulls—
Egrets hunting in the tidal shallows, a ribbon
Of sandpipers fluttering over mudflats, white,
Then not. A drift of mist wisping off the bay.
This is the moment when bliss is what you glimpse
From the corner of your eye, as you drive past
Running errands, and the wind comes up,
And the surface of the water glitters hard against it.

NOTES

"WINGED AND ACID DARK": "Potsdamerplatz, May, 1945." See Anonymous, *A Woman in Berlin: Eight Weeks in a Conquered City*, translated by Philip Boehm, Metropolitan Books, 2005.

"ART AND LIFE": Vermeer's *Woman Pouring Milk* can be seen at the Rijksmuseum in Amsterdam, but I have a distinct memory of having seen it in The Hague at the Mauritshuis Museum in 1976. Perhaps it was on loan. In any case, I have been faithful to my memory.

"TOMAS TRANSTRÖMER: SONG": In 1986, when I edited Tomas Tranströmer's *Selected Poems* for Ecco Press, I was able to include sixteen poems from his first book, called in Swedish *17 Dikter*. The seventeenth poem, "Song," could not be included because it was written in a fairly regular blank verse, and Mr. Tranströmer was not interested in free verse approximations. This attempt at the poem depends on literal translations supplied to me by Joanna Bankier and Marta de Marothy. "Vainomoinen" is a figure from Baltic mythology, the hero of the Finnish epic cycle, the *Kalevala*. I have included my translation here for the contrast it provides to the ways of thinking about the natural world in "State of the Planet."

"I AM YOUR WAITER TONIGHT AND MY NAME IS DMITRI": Fyodor Dostoyevsky mistakenly describes Grushenka—in the Constance Garnett translation—as a "brunette." Alfred Nobel died in 1896. His German company *Dynamikatiengesellschaft* (DAG) and its subsidiaries, including the Nobel-Dynamite Trust Company in London, manufactured munitions, as did Bofors, the Swedish armaments company he owned until his death.

"A POEM": "Leon Goure": See Frances FitzGerald, *Fire in the Lake: The Vietnamese and the Americans in Vietnam*, Boston: Atlantic, Little, Brown, 1972, pp. 166–167.
" . . . whole races of tropical birds": see *The Air War in Indochina*, ed. Raphael Littauer and Norman Uphoff, Air War Study Group, Cornell University, revised edition, Boston: Beacon Press, 1972, pp. 94–95, 256–260. Also, generally, Sven Lindqvist, *A History of Bombing*, translated by Linda Haverty Rugg, New York: New Press, 2000.